Trae Young: The Inspiring Story of One of Basketball's Star Guards

An Unauthorized Biography

HAPPY 9TH
Birthday

love,

aunt mary

By: Clayton Geoffreys

Table of Contents

Foreword 1

Introduction 3

Chapter 1: Childhood and Early Life 12

Chapter 2: High School Career 21

Chapter 3: College Career 31

Chapter 4: NBA Career 40

Getting Drafted...40

Early Jitters, Race for Rookie of the Year 57

Rise to Stardom 83

Chapter 5: Personal Life.....................................104

Chapter 6: Legacy and Future 107

Final Word/About the Author 112

References 116

Foreword

When Stephen Curry rose through the ranks to become one of the elite point guards in the NBA, it was only a matter of time before pundits wondered how Steph's game would impact future guards in the NBA. The game of basketball has rapidly evolved in recent years, turning many games into three-point shoot outs where teams win and lose games behind the three-point line. It would be tough to argue that Trae Young's entrance into the NBA and quick ascension as one of the latest generation's star point guards wasn't made possible because of Steph Curry's earlier breakthroughs. Trae's game is in many regards similar to Steph's, with at times even more audacity as Trae has been known to nutmeg his opponents when the opportunities arise. It'll be exciting to see Trae's career continue to develop. At the time of this writing, Young is wrapping up his second regular season and already an NBA All-Star. Thank you for purchasing *Trae Young: The Inspiring Story of One of Basketball's Star Guards*.

In this unauthorized biography, we will learn Trae Young's incredible life story and impact on the game of basketball. Hope you enjoy and if you do, please do not forget to leave a review!

Also, check out my website at claytongeoffreys.com to join my exclusive list where I let you know about my latest books. To thank you for your purchase, you can go to my site to download a free copy of *33 Life Lessons: Success Principles, Career Advice & Habits of Successful People.* In the book, you'll learn from some of the greatest thought leaders of different industries on what it takes to become successful and how to live a great life.

Cheers,

Clayton Geoffreys

Visit me at www.claytongeoffreys.com

Introduction

As the famous saying goes, "We are a product of our time." This is true wherever you go, as different things and people are merely who and what they are because the trends and events of their time shaped them to be so. Think about it. If you imagine yourself living in a different generation, say, for example, 50 years ago, you would surely be someone a lot different than who you are today. That is what it means to be a product of your time.

The same goes for the world of basketball. Players are merely a product of their time in the sense that they are shaped by the star players they look up to and by the trends in the biggest basketball leagues in the world. After all, as they say, basketball is a copycat sport. Younger players will always look up to the best players in the world and try to model their games after them. That is how most of the players of our time have been built.

Kids who grew up during the 80s and the 90s wanted to be like Magic Johnson. That is why the NBA saw an influx of big guards during the 90s as Jason Kidd, Penny Hardaway, and Gary Payton all watched and learned from Magic. In the same way, even bigger players playing different positions learned how to play that all-around style. Kevin Garnett idolized Magic Johnson more than any other player while he was growing up, even though he played the power forward spot.

In the 90s, many kids began idolizing Michael Jordan. They loved that isolation style of basketball that saw them making a series of moves with their feet to get a difficult shot off over the outstretched arms of their defenders. The late great Kobe Bryant grew up watching Jordan and became the closest thing we could ever have to him. We also had a lot of high-scoring and high-flying wings such as Vince Carter, Tracy McGrady, and Paul Pierce playing stellar basketball during the 2000s precisely because they grew up during the Jordan era.

During the middle to latter part of the 2010s, we saw an influx of position-less players that all have a complete set of basketball skills. They can dribble, pass, and shoot regardless of whatever position they play. LeBron James, because of how he basically broke the rules of basketball by playing any position, was the pioneer of this position-less style of play. That is why plenty of basketball players right now can actually do everything.

When it comes to the newest age of basketball players, one name, Steph Curry, usually comes to mind when discussing how the game being played has changed. Other than the fact that the best players we see today are all skilled in every facet of the game and can play practically any position, we are now seeing an influx of players that are shooting more and more three-pointers. Steph Curry's three-point play has had an immense, dynamic influence on the way the game has evolved into what it is now. Other players such as Klay Thompson and Damian Lillard are also some of the big names when it comes to the three-point shot.

The NBA is also a league of trends. Teams follow the styles of other teams that have shown a lot of success in the way they play. That is why plenty of teams now focus on spacing and ball movement, as the 2014 San Antonio Spurs and the Golden State Warriors championship dynasty have proven that pairing ball movement with three-point shooting makes a winning formula. At times, statistics also go into play as we have seen how the Houston Rockets of the late 2010s have focused only on layups and three-point shooting.

All those factors—the success of players shooting more three-pointers and the championship victories of teams that shoot three-pointers—have factored into the current generation of players that are making their way into the league. For many people, the first standout product of the Steph Curry three-point era is arguably the All-Star guard named Trae Young.

If you look at Trae Young, he is a lot like Curry in the sense that he does not look like he could become a star player or even excel in the sport of basketball. In a game where height is might, Young is shorter than most point guards today. On top of that, he is a scrawny player and an average athlete in a league that has big and athletic point guards such as Russell Westbrook, John Wall, and Ben Simmons. But, just like Curry, he was able to make a name for himself by making full use of basketball's most dangerous weapon—the three-point shot.

Trae Young basically spent his high school career watching how Stephen Curry helped change the game of basketball using the three-point shot. Curry and the Warriors won the NBA title in 2015 when Young was still a sophomore. Later on, other guards in the NBA began shooting the three-pointer with ever-increasing skill and precision by doing so in split seconds from off the dribble and even several feet beyond the three-point line. In that sense, Trae Young was a witness to how the game of basketball changed because of the three-point shot. And he was lucky enough that it happened during a time when Young was still developing.

Using the three-pointer to his advantage, Trae Young was able to make up for his lack of size and athleticism. In high school, he was destroying other teams using the three-point shot. He was even doing it from well beyond the arc. On top of that, he was also able to take his cue from Curry by mixing up his offensive game with a good balance of layups and floaters. This allowed Trae Young to average over 40 points a game during his senior year as a prep athlete despite his apparent lack of height and his slight frame.

Known mainly as a scorer during his high school years, Trae Young came to the University of Oklahoma as a five-star athlete thanks to his ability to put up points on the scoreboard and drain the three-point shot. But what the entire nation did not realize at the time was that he was as capable a point guard as any other when it came to making plays for others. Young tore up the collegiate ranks and was not only putting up ridiculous scoring numbers but was also leading the entire nation in assists.

At the end of his collegiate career as a freshman, Trae Young was the first-ever player to lead the nation in points and assists in a single season. He did so using the three-pointer to open other scoring opportunities while also using his playmaking skills to make the game easier for his teammates. Young was destroying records as a freshman and was winning individual awards on his way to becoming one of the most highly touted prospects of that year's NBA draft.

Even though Young was possibly the best college player that season, he still had doubters as he was coming into the NBA. He did not have the size or athletic skills that some of the best guards in the league had at that time. And while he was still a top-five player heading into the draft, he was overlooked in favor of other prospects.

But Trae Young went on to prove that he was an NBA-caliber player. After struggling a bit during the earlier portion of his first season, he eventually recovered during the second half and became one of the most fantastic rookies in recent memory. He was putting up amazing shooting and scoring numbers while also leading the rookies in assists. Even though another rookie named Luka Dončić was regarded as the runaway and unanimous winner for the Rookie of the Year Award, Young closed the gap and made the race for that accolade a bit closer.

Trae Young did indeed end up losing to Dončić for the Rookie of the Year Award but he was second in scoring and first in assists among all rookies. Had the draft been done all over again, he could have been the second overall pick. And had he adjusted to the NBA style a bit earlier in the season, he could have made the Rookie of the Year race tighter than it was. Young essentially proved his doubters wrong.

The following season, Trae Young made a huge jump in terms of his individual production. He proved that he was a star on the rise, as he was able to put in the necessary work that allowed him to average 29 points and 9 assists. Young, at the age of 21, became an All-Star starter for the Eastern Conference. At that point, it was becoming apparent that he was going to be one of the young players that would lead the NBA into the future.

Doubted for a good majority of his young life due to his lack of size and athletic gifts, Trae Young is the picture of hard work and perseverance. He is the product of a time that favored players such as him, as he was able to make use of the new rules and trends in the NBA to make the three-pointer as dangerous a weapon as it has always been. And while he is yet to prove himself in the league as one of the best shooters and players, he is already on the rise and could very well reach the level of all-time great shooters at the point guard spot such as Steph Curry and Damian Lillard. And with the work he is putting himself through, he might even reach greater heights.

Chapter 1: Childhood and Early Life

Rayford Trae Young was born on September 19, 1998, in Lubbock, Texas. He is the eldest of four siblings, with a younger brother and two younger sisters. Named after his father, Trae is the son of Rayford Young, who was also a good basketball player in his own right after playing college ball in Texas Tech and spending time overseas as a professional in Europe. Trae Young's mother is Candice Young.

Trae Young and his family would soon move to Norman, Oklahoma, where he would eventually become a legend in his own right not only in the town but in the entire state as well. However, at that time, he was still just a young boy trying to learn how to play basketball. And, at the time he was born, his father Rayford was still a junior at Texas Tech.[i]

Rayford and Candice were high school sweethearts who both went to college at Texas Tech. Candice got pregnant with Trae when Rayford was still heading into his junior season as a collegiate basketball player with the school's basketball team. At that time, he was a star for Texas Tech and was seemingly a similar type of player to what his son Trae would soon become.

Rayford Young was a pretty good guard himself back when he was still at Texas Tech. At 5'11", he was an undersized point guard but was still very much capable of holding his own against all the other collegiate point guards during his time with the team. He had an underwhelming freshman year but went on to become a solid backcourt scorer in the next three seasons. As a senior, Rayford Young averaged 17.8 points, 4.2 assists, and 1.8 steals while making 2 of his 5.6 three-point shot attempts per game.

With his lack of size and because of his natural ability to shoot and score the ball even as an undersized point guard, Rayford Young was the prelude of what his son was going to become. He did not have the range of Trae at that time, but he was a capable shooter himself. Unfortunately, after he finished his playing years with Texas Tech, he was unable to get to the NBA primarily because of his lack of size.

Trae was about two years old when his dad finished playing college basketball. However, Rayford's basketball aspirations did not end there. He found a career playing overseas as a professional basketball player in Europe. At the time, Candice had just given birth to Caitlyn, Trae's younger sister. The couple toured all over Europe while Candice brought the toddlers, Trae and Caitlyn, to see their father play.[i]

Watching his dad in his stints as a professional point guard in countries such as Portugal, Spain, France, and Italy, Trae Young was groomed to become a basketball player from his earliest moments, as he was pretty much born into the sport and spent his most formative years surrounded by and growing into the sport.

After Rayford's playing days in Europe were done, the family decided to move back to the United States. But instead of staying in Texas, where the couple met and where Trae was born, they decided to settle in Norman, Oklahoma because they wanted to be close to Candice's family there. It was in Norman where Trae Young learned the basics of basketball with his father teaching him the fundamentals of the game—dribbling, passing, and shooting. But, at that time, he probably did not know that those same fundamentals were the very tools that would help him succeed in the sport.

Rayford knew for a fact that Trae needed to be in a place that would allow him to become more competitive in the sport if he wanted to excel as a basketball player. That is why he made it a point to put in the necessary time and effort into helping his son develop his talent and natural pedigree. He dedicated himself to driving Trae for three to six hours to Texas to try to immerse his son in a more competitive playing field. As early as Trae's grade school years, Rayford often asked him if he wanted to have fun playing with his friends in Norman, or if he wanted to become one of the very best. The hours spent driving Trae back and forth to Dallas and even Houston proved to one of Rayford's biggest sacrifices for his son back then.

Aside from spending hours and hours traveling all the way to Texas just to find better competition, the father-and-son duo also spent a lot of time watching videos of players. Living in Norman proved to be a good thing for the family because they were merely half an hour away from Oklahoma City, the city the Thunder have been calling home since 2008. Ever since the Seattle

SuperSonics relocated to Oklahoma to become the Thunder, Rayford made it a point to purchase season tickets for the family.

But Trae and Rayford were not watching OKC Thunder games just for the fun of it. As a point guard himself, Rayford spent time breaking down what he was seeing on the court to help his son's development. They would go to the arena hours before the start of the game just so they could watch the Thunder players' pre-game routine. Rayford thought that Trae could learn to mimic the routine so that he could potentially incorporate those practices into his own game.[i]

Luckily for Trae Young, his father had spent years forming relationships with former players who were able to get jobs in different NBA teams. Rayford managed to contact his friends and get ahold of several DVDs of various players. He spliced the videos together so that Trae could have something he could watch and learn from. Some of those videos included

Kyrie Irving's pre-draft workouts as well as Warriors games.[i] At that time, Steph Curry was already playing for Golden State.

Watching Kyrie Irving's videos and routine allowed Trae to train his ball-handling skills as early as possible. His father was only 5'11" and the entire family was well aware that Trae probably was not going to outgrow his father by much. That was the reason why there was a need for him to develop good handles at the point guard spot, which was probably the only position he could play.

However, Rayford was also well-aware that Trae was going to need more offensive tools that could help him finish near the basket when he gets away from his man off the dribble. As small and unathletic as he was, he needed to develop a weapon that could make up for his lack of size. Rayford helped Trae develop a floater that was patterned after Steve Nash's own floater.

Training to become a future NBA player needed hard work and dedication on the part of both father and son. They trained almost every single day, even during school days. Sessions started in the local YMCA at 6 a.m. and then Trae would return to the gym after school. The young boy learned how to make the floater his own through the rigorous training sessions he had with his dad. But since Rayford was not too tall himself, he needed to use a broom to simulate the outstretched arms of a shot-blocking big man inside the paint.[i]

While a lot of today's veteran players grew up watching Kobe Bryant highlights and learning a thing or two from him and other players such as LeBron James and Dwyane Wade, Trae Young was a product of the point guard explosion that started during the latter part of the 2000s. He grew up watching the best point guards in the NBA and was inspired by other small and seemingly unathletic guys such as Kyrie Irving, Stephen Curry, and Steve Nash, who were able to do well in the league despite their apparent weaknesses. Young could not have asked for a better era to grow up in.

Developing his skills at an early age involved an environment that was somewhat reminiscent of a drill camp for both Trae and Rayford. The local YMCA had three courts, and the two of them occupied one. In the other courts were children the same age as Trae, but they were merely having fun with their dads shooting the ball and laughing around. Trae and Rayford were the only ones serious about what they were doing most of the time because the older Young knew what kind of hard work was needed to get his son to the level that could give him a chance at an NBA career. Needless to say, Trae Young was certainly groomed to make it to the big leagues ever since he was a young boy.

Looking back at what he experienced when he was still a young boy, Trae Young said that he was lucky to have his father by his side when he was still developing. Not a lot of future NBA players grew up with fathers like his, and some, no fathers at all. And among those who indeed had fathers in their lives, Trae Young was one of the few to have a dad who took an active role in helping him succeed as a basketball player.[ii] Rayford might not have made it to the NBA himself, but Trae Young's success was his success.

Chapter 2: High School Career

Armed with ball-handling skills he learned from watching Kyrie Irving videos over and over again, a shooting form reminiscent of Steph Curry's, and a floater that was patterned after Steve Nash's, Trae Young was heading into high school as the ultimate scoring point guard with all the offensive tools you would need from a player at that position. Best of all, he had the confidence and competitive mentality drilled into him by his dad ever since he was young.

Trae Young started high school in 2013 when he enrolled in a local hometown high school, Norman North High School, based out of Norman, Oklahoma. Young did not play on the varsity team during his first year of high school but he was the freshman team's best player. As a freshman, he was averaging 24 points a game and was seemingly the complete package at the point guard position as far as scoring was concerned.

The following year, Trae Young made the Norman North High School basketball team and was given the starting point guard spot. He did not disappoint as a sophomore. As short and as scrawny as he was back then, Young proved that he did not need to be over six feet tall or close to 200 pounds to make a big difference as a scorer. Instead, he let his skills do the talking as he was able to average amazing numbers of 25 points, 4 rebounds, and 5 assists during his sophomore year. For a player to dominate the scoring end at such a young age was already very impressive.

During the middle of Trae's sophomore year, he was already getting a lot of recruitment offers from reputable college programs all over the country. That was also another impressive feat because most players get recruited during their junior year. Young was already showing a lot of maturity at that time to the point that college programs were already interested in him. He was able to lead his team to the 2015 area championship game and earned himself the Oklahoma Sophomore of the Year Award.

By the time he was a junior during the 2015-16 season, Trae Young had blossomed into an even scarier offensive threat for Norman North High School. He upped his stats to dazzling numbers of 34.2 points, 4.6 rebounds, and 4.6 assists per game. Young shot his way to a regional title for his school. He even led his team to a runner-up finish in the 2016 Oklahoma Class 6A championship game. As such, Young was easily the best young player in the entire state and was named Oklahoma's Player of the Year by almost all the writers in that area. But just when everyone thought he had peaked, Trae Young proved that he was still far away from realizing his full potential.

Entering his senior year during the 2016-17 season, Trae Young was already a witness to how much the game of basketball had changed in the NBA. It was during the 2014-15 season when Stephen Curry won his first MVP title and went on to lead the Golden State Warriors to the first of their three NBA titles over the course of the next four NBA finals. And while Curry won the very first unanimous MVP title after upping his game to average 30 a night in the NBA while leading the Warriors to a record-breaking 73-win season during the 2016-17 season, he and his team squandered away a 3-1 series lead in the finals.

Still, Steph Curry was regarded as one of the top five players in the NBA. All of the other five players were either athletic or big or were a combination of both. Curry was neither, yet he won back-to-back MVP awards and became the first unanimous winner of that accolade. And how did he do it? By using the three-pointer to his advantage.

At that point, Trae had already seen how Steph Curry changed the game of basketball by maximizing the capabilities of the three-point shot. He could shoot the ball off the dribble in a split second just after seeing a small opening. He moves around the court so well while finding screens set for him just to get an open shot. And the best part was that Stephen Curry was pulling up more than 30 feet away from the basket but was still making his shots at an incredibly accurate rate. Curry was not alone in that department as other shooters such as James Harden and Damian Lillard have also learned to maximize the three-pointer while shooting it from ridiculous distances.

Trae Young did not need to get to the NBA to develop a knack for shooting distant three-pointers. When everyone else in high school thought that he had already shown his full potential, Young made sure that he was still very much developing as he incorporated the long three-point shot into his game. By the time he became a senior, Young was confidently pulling up from 30 feet without even showing any hint of hesitation. The moment he crossed the half-court line, he was already in range.

Even those who were not following Oklahoma basketball games were introduced to Trae Young's awesome accuracy as a three-point shooter when videos of his highlights surfaced on the internet. The videos proved that Young was indeed pulling up and making shots from distances only guys like Curry and Lillard were capable of shooting from. This was what prompted basketball fans all over the world to dub Trae Young the "next coming of Stephen Curry."

As impressive as Trae's junior year was, he was even more impressive during his senior season when he went on to average 42.6 points, 5.8 rebounds, and 4.1 assists. At one point, he even scored a state-record of 62 points against Edmond Memorial.[iii] It was already elementary that Trae Young was going to be one of the most highly-touted prospects heading into college. He earned himself dozens of recruitment offers as early as his sophomore season but he waited until 2017 to make a decision.

Trae Young, even after averaging more than 42 points a game during his senior year, was not the highest-rated player or even the top point guard of his recruitment class. In fact, *ESPN* listed him as the 23rd best player of the 2017 recruitment class. He was also regarded as the third-best point guard behind Collin Sexton and Jaylen Hands, both of whom were also able to get drafted into the NBA.[iv] Nevertheless, Young was still a five-star recruit according to all the reputable sources in the country. That was why he was highly recruited by a lot of good college programs at the end of his senior year.

Before he went to college, Trae needed to make a decision. He narrowed his choices down to a few reputable programs. Rayford Young made his son think about going to Texas Tech because that was where he and Candice had attended. However, Texas Tech was not really the most competitive school at that point in time. That was why Rayford implored his son to go to Kentucky instead.

Kentucky and their head coach, John Calipari, have a history of producing some of the best stars in the NBA. Names such as Anthony Davis, Karl-Anthony Towns, and Bam Adebayo are some of the best big men that Calipari has produced. However, his system is even better at producing All-Star guards and high-quality backcourt players. Guards such as John Wall, Devin Booker, De'Aaron Fox, and Jamal Murray are all Kentucky products. Based on that list, Young felt he had a chance to develop into an All-Star under Calipari's tutelage in Kentucky.[i]

But while Rayford preferred Kentucky, Candice wanted her son to choose a school closer to home instead and told her son to go to Kansas, which was only about four hours away from Norman. However, both Rayford and Candice gave their eldest son the freedom to choose where he wanted to make a name for himself and develop into a stellar guard.

Trae Young, having been raised in Norman, Oklahoma, had already gotten to know all the players in the entire state. He even formed a good bond with the University of Oklahoma players by playing pickup games with them. The University of Oklahoma was based in Norman, which would allow Trae Young to stay at home. As such, he chose the comforts of home and the relationship he had formed with his friends over bigger college programs known for recruiting five-star prospects.

With that, Trae Young became the Oklahoma Sooners' first five-star recruit since 2010. And while Oklahoma did not stand out in the collegiate ranks and was not a top team in one of the most competitive conferences in the country, Trae Young grew up and developed into a player that had the confidence to know that he could still turn into a star no matter where he played. So, in hindsight, he could have chosen Kentucky or Kansas, but the end result was still going to be the same. Choosing Oklahoma only allowed Trae Young to shine as one of the brightest collegiate stars in the entire nation.

Chapter 3: College Career

Trae Young joined an Oklahoma Sooners team that was not exactly known for producing the best basketball talents. Since producing Blake Griffin, the program had only been able to produce two other NBA players. And in the last five years before securing Young, the only Oklahoma player to make it to the NBA was Buddy Hield. Griffin and Hield are the only other Oklahoma products with roster spots in the NBA as of this writing. In other words, this was not one of the top schools to go to if you wanted to become a future NBA player. But that did not stop the rising point guard from wanting to make his mark with the school he personally chose to go to.

When Oklahoma (and probably the rest of the nation) recruited Trae Young, what they saw was a pure scorer from the point guard position. Barely 6'2" and weighing a bit over 150 pounds going into college, this was an undersized and scrawny kid who did not look like he could stand out in basketball but impressively averaged almost 43 points a night as a high school senior because of his complete scoring abilities. He was built like Steph Curry and also had the skill set that allowed him to play like the two-time MVP.

Trae Young was a complete scorer at his position and Oklahoma needed that scoring punch. But the problem was that Young was playing the point guard role. Traditionally, point guards are known to be playmakers and passers rather than scorers. Times have changed and the point guard role in the NBA has now evolved into a score-first role with the likes of Steph Curry, Kyrie Irving, Damian Lillard, and Russell Westbrook opting to score first rather than pass. Nevertheless, those players are also known for being terrific playmakers in their own right. That was not the case for Trae when he entered college because of how he barely averaged five dimes in high school. But people got him all wrong.

Similarly to the way he surprised everyone in high school when he incorporated the long three-pointer into his arsenal, Trae Young was once again impressing observers when he began to showcase how good of a playmaker he truly was. In his first game for Oklahoma, he struggled as a scorer when he finished with just 12 points on a 4 out of 13 shooting clip. However, what amazed everyone was that he finished with 10 assists in that win over Omaha on November 12, 2017. And when everyone thought that was a fluke, he finished a win over Ball State three days later with 22 points and 13 assists. That was merely the start of what was going to be a Trae Young show all season long.

After going for 33 points against Portland in a nationally-televised game on November 24th, Young finished with 43 ridiculous points against Oregon. And after that game, he went on to destroy North Texas with 32 points and 10 assists. Soon after that, Trae Young was in full force as an offensive threat that could practically do anything you would ask from a star point guard.

Trae Young heard the criticisms about his game and that he was more focused on scoring than on making plays for others, like any point guard should be doing. With that freshly in mind, he did not even attempt a lot of baskets for himself against Northwestern State on December 19th. Instead, he was more focused on setting his teammates up for 22 big assists in addition to the 26 points he had.

At that point, there was no arguing the fact that Trae Young was already a true point guard in both the traditional and the new sense of the position. He could set himself up for scoring opportunities regardless of where he was on the floor. But, at the same time, he was showing a facet of his game many scouts thought he did not possess back when he was in high school.

In college, Young was setting teammates up for shot opportunities they did not even know they had. He regularly threaded needles to make tough passes from long distances and was doing it with either hand. And following that 22-assist game, Trae Young went for three more double-double performances to record five consecutive games of double-digit scoring and assisting.

When asked if playmaking was something he consciously worked on before he got to the collegiate level, Trae simply said that the reason why he became such a prolific passer in college was the change of perception. The young point guard, knowing that he was going to be asked to make plays for a team that did not have a lot of talent, made it a point to put in the necessary effort on the playmaking side of his game. But, at the same time, he was just a complete offensive point guard.

On January 13, 2018, Trae Young showcased his all-around prowess against TCU in what was a hard-fought win for Oklahoma. He finished that game by tying his college career high of 43 points while barely missing a triple-double after tallying 11 rebounds and 7 assists. He also hit 10 three-pointers in the entire game. That was Trae Young's finest all-around performance that season but he was still on his way to putting up more high-scoring performances for the Sooners.

In a loss to rival school Oklahoma State on January 20th, Trae Young pushed himself to the limit and came out with 48 points while making 14 of his 39 shots and 8 of his 20 three-point attempts. Adding one more 40-point scoring game to his name that season, Young finished a win over Baylor on January 30th with 44 points and 9 assists. He hit 16 of his 19 free throws in that contest.

Trae Young helped the Oklahoma Sooners to a winning season after spending a few years as one of the worst teams in the Big 12. The Sooners even made it as far as the NCAA Tournament but eventually bowed out of the tourney in just the first round. In that loss to Rhode Island, Young finished with 28 points, 5 rebounds, and 7 assists. The only other freshman to have similar numbers in an NCAA game was Chris Paul, who was able to accomplish that feat nearly a decade and a half ago.

At the end of what was a spectacular freshman season, Trae Young led the entire nation in points and assists to become the first player in NCAA history to accomplish that feat. He finished with 27.4 points, 3.9 rebounds, and 8.7 assists while shooting 36% from the three-point area. And proving that he was not merely a shooter but also a player with an attacking mentality, Young ended the season hitting 7.4 of his 8.6 free throw attempts per game.

Trae received plenty of accolades at the end of what was one of the greatest freshman seasons a point guard could ever have. He was named the National Freshman Player of the Year by the USBWA, the Big 12

Freshman of the Year, and an All-Big 12 First Team member. Young was also one of three other freshmen to be named into the All-American First Team. Despite having been overlooked for being undersized, Young managed to dominate the collegiate ranks in his own special way.

Because of what he was doing in college all season long, Trae Young received a lot of praise from some of the greatest players in the world. Steph Curry, the man he was often compared to because of their similar style of play, said that the younger shooter-passer was having one of the most unbelievable seasons and also pointed out how great Young was at being such a magnetic presence. Russell Westbrook also said something along the lines. Even LeBron James could not help but hop onto the Trae Young hype train after he posted some photos of him and Young in a training camp. All of those players won MVP trophies in the NBA, but they were still in awe at what Young was able to accomplish.

Ready for the NBA after spending a single season in college, Trae Young announced that he was going to forego his three remaining seasons in Oklahoma to pursue the dream and the career he had been readying himself for and had been groomed for by his father ever since he was old enough to hold a ball in his hands. With all the fantastic individual performances he put up during college, Trae Young had the hype, talent, and production that made him one of the hottest commodities during the 2018 NBA Draft.

Chapter 4: NBA Career

Getting Drafted

When Trae Young announced that he was going to take part in the 2018 NBA Draft following what was regarded one of the greatest seasons of all time by a freshman, he officially became one of the high-profile names in one of the best draft classes in recent memory in terms of the talent and potential of the players vying for a slot on an NBA team.

Trae Young was not the only standout freshman entering the draft as it also featured notables Deandre Ayton and Marvin Bagley, who were also named to the All-American First Team as freshmen. Ayton and Bagley both averaged 20 points and 11 rebounds as freshmen and were playing for better teams. On top of that, as athletic seven-footers, they seemed to be better-equipped than Trae Young as far as physical capabilities were concerned. That was why Ayton was regarded as the consensus first pick for the 2018 NBA

Draft. Meanwhile, Bagley was also a player who was slated to be chosen within the top three of that year's draft.

Other than Ayton and Bagley, there were also other notable names that were regarded as top prospects thanks to their combination of talent, potential, and physical gifts. The seven-footer Mohamed Bamba's record-breaking 7'10" wingspan made him an intriguing prospect. The 18-year old Jaren Jackson Jr., son of former NBA player and coach Jaren Jackson Sr., had the talent and skill level that made him a unique player. And then there were guys such as Wendell Carter Jr., Collin Sexton, Kevin Knox, and Shai Gilgeous-Alexander who also made the draft so interesting.

Another intriguing player, albeit one that not many scouts thought would run out of the gates strong, was the Slovenian basketball genius named Luka Dončić, who dominated the European leagues and went on to win the EuroLeague MVP at the tender age of 18. As talented as Dončić was, what many scouts believed kept him away from the top spot of that year's NBA draft was that he did not have the athleticism of some of the other prospects. Moreover, he was also somewhat of a mystery because the European leagues are much different compared to the collegiate ranks in the United States. Nevertheless, Dončić was still regarded as one of the top prospects of that draft.

With all those talented names and prospects flooding the list with their combination of skill, potential, and physical attributes, one would wonder where Trae Young ranked among them. Was he one of the best players coming into the NBA draft or were his numbers in college inflated because he might simply be considered a good player playing for a bad team?

Well, it turned out that Young was indeed regarded as one of the top players in the draft and was most likely going to be taken within the top five. The reason was that he was simply too talented to pass up for any team picking in the top five that year. Of course, it helps to know more about Young's scouting report to understand why scouts were so high on him.

As a dribbler, there was no denying that Trae Young was already as complete as you could get. He came into the draft and even into college with dribbling skills that were at NBA-level. His handles were already as tight as any player and were reminiscent of what Kyrie Irving could do at the highest level. He could do hesitation dribbles that allowed him to get his defenders off-balance and create space for himself. His shiftiness with his handles made it almost impossible for defenders at the college level to stay in front of him. And of course, his ability to dribble into the lane with ease made it possible for Young to pick apart defenses either in isolation situations or when playing the pick-and-roll.[v]

Trae Young's ability to dribble opened up a lot of the other facets of his college game in the same way his ability to shoot from the floor opened up his ability to get to the basket with his dribble moves.

Speaking of shooting, that was always the part of Young's game that made him an exciting prospect to watch even when he was still in high school. Earning himself comparisons to Stephen Curry, Trae Young was already a masterful shooter back in high school. When players like Curry and Lillard were beginning to shoot distance-defining three-pointers in the NBA during the middle of the 2010s, Young followed suit and was doing it at the high school level and eventually brought the same kind of extended-range shooting to college.

Trae Young was basically owning the college ranks because of his ability to sink the long-range shot. While there were other shooters who were impressing scouts by shooting three-pointers from the NBA distance in college, Young was putting on offensive shows by shooting three-pointers from several feet behind the NBA three-point line. This allowed him to sink a total of 118 three-point shots back in college.

But Trae Young's ability to hit three-pointers is not a function of him running around the floor looking for screens to get himself open, much like how Klay Thompson, Ray Allen, and Reggie Miller freed themselves up for an open three. Instead, Young was just as likely to shoot the three off the dribble as he was off the catch. A lot of his three-point shots came off the dribble because he was the Oklahoma Sooners' designated ball-handler. He was making use of isolation plays and pick-and-roll plays to get an open shot off the bounce.

And when he did not have the ball in his hands, Young also showed excellent instincts in finding an open spot for himself to get a clear look at the basket. As an off-the-dribble shooter, Young was in the 88th percentile.

When shooting off the catch, he ranked within the 96th percentile. Those numbers show how good Trae Young was as a shooter, regardless of whether it was off the bounce or off the catch.

Trae Young's shooting form and release is also a facet of his game that allowed him to excel as a shooter. He does not have the picture-perfect Klay Thompson form but he did have a compact release similar to Curry's in the sense that it is quick, efficient, and easy for him to pull. Young was able to shoot baskets quickly off the dribble without wasting any kind of motion that would have allowed defenders to recover on him.[vi]

Shooting was not the only facet of Trae Young's game that made him such a deadly scorer in college. Much like Steph Curry, Young's ability to shoot opened a lot of opportunities for him to use his dribbling skills to get to the basket. Defenders were quick to close out on him because they feared his unlimited shooting range. When he drove, he used hesitation moves, in and out dribbles, and shifty moves that made it possible for him to break defenses down and get to the basket. And when Young got to the basket, he was able to show his aggressiveness as a finisher.

Making use of runners or floaters was Young's specialty when finishing near the basket. He perfected a floater that he patterned after Steve Nash's so that he could still finish over bigger and stronger defenders near the paint. But, seeing how he was shooting nine free throws a game in college, it was clear that Trae was not afraid to attack defenders or to use his body to draw fouls when trying to go up for a layup.

As a point guard, Trae Young also had the responsibility of not only creating scoring opportunities for himself but also making sure that his teammates were in a position to excel offensively. He was not regarded as a true point guard as he entered college but he changed perceptions rather quickly by showing his willingness to add a different dimension to his game by becoming a more complete passer.

Trae Young passes the ball like a true point guard. On top of that, he is willing to pass at any given possession and he always keeps his head up to find teammates while also finding the best shot opportunities for himself. But if he had a teammate with a better shot, Young would always defer by passing the ball for an assist. And Trae Young's high assist numbers were not merely a product of how often he had the ball in his hands. Instead, he was making all sorts of passes and was unafraid to try to thread needles just so he could give teammates open shots. And by using his shooting range and dribbling skills, it was easy for him to break defenses down. This made him a masterful passer off the pick-and-roll as well as when he attracted multiple defenders.

Offensively, there were not a lot of problems in Trae Young's game when he was entering the 2018 NBA

Draft. He was as complete a point guard in terms of the offensive skills that he had at that point in his career. And completing his overall abilities on offense was his mindset. Young had the confidence that allowed him to feel like he could do anything on the floor. His mentality made it possible for him to overcome other weaknesses.

And speaking of weaknesses, Trae Young was anything but a perfect player, however, because he also had some downsides to his game and to the overall package he brought to the table. Such weaknesses were what kept him from becoming the undisputed best player of his draft class.

For one, size was arguably Trae Young's biggest weakness. Standing close to 6'2" and weighing about 175 pounds, the Sooners point guard did not have a lot of size. The NBA is no stranger to shorter guards standing somewhere close to six feet. Allen Iverson led the league in scoring numerous times despite being thin and barely six feet tall. In the modern era, Chris Paul, Kyle Lowry, and Kemba Walker became All-Star point guards at about six feet tall. Even Stephen Curry, with his skinny 6'3" frame, is now one of the greatest players in the NBA despite him being one of the smaller superstars in the league.

In Trae Young's case, however, he was not only an undersized guard but also lacked the physicality and the athleticism that allowed some of the other point guards in the NBA to excel. What Chris Paul, Kyle Lowry, and Kemba Walker lacked in height they made up in their strong frame and quickness. But Trae Young did not have the body frame of a Chris Paul and was coming into the league with subpar athletic abilities. As shifty as he may be, Young did not have the quickness of a Kyrie Irving, the footspeed of a John Wall, or the nuclear explosiveness of a Russell Westbrook. In that regard, Young was looking like a smaller version of Steph Curry.

At the start of his collegiate career, Trae Young was able to make use of his complete skill set to score at will. But as the season went by, teams began to find out that using a physical approach was the right way to defend the Oklahoma star point guard. One case in point was when Trae matched up with his fellow 2018 NBA Draft classmate Collin Sexton, who is by no means much bigger than the Sooners star.

Collin Sexton, who was regarded as one of the best point guards of that draft class, was one of the other prospects high on the list of a lot of teams that season. At about 6'2" and 180 pounds, he is not much larger than Trae. But Sexton was able to bully Young in their matchup in college by using his superior strength on both offense and defense to make life difficult for the Sooners star.

Defensively, Trae Young also got himself exposed in that matchup against Sexton as his lack of strength and his inability to keep up laterally made it possible for his opponent to easily drive past him on numerous occasions. On top of that, Young's wingspan is below average and will not help him on the defensive end of the floor. Faster players can drive past him while taller and longer scorers can merely shoot over him.

Trae's lack of size, strength, and athleticism could possibly make it harder for him to score against bigger and more athletic defenders in the NBA. He might have eaten defenses alive in college, but defenders in the NBA are bigger, faster, stronger, and smarter than the ones he faced when he was still in Oklahoma.

If a strong defender like Marcus Smart or Patrick Beverley were to defend him in an entire game, it would be difficult for Young to shoot long-distance threes with his defender crowding him the moment he passes the half-court line. He could also get the Steph Curry treatment as defenders might blitz and trap him the moment he touches the ball. If he did indeed get to the basket, he would have to try to score up against longer and more agile rim protectors. And the problem with Young was that he only shot jumpers when they were from the three-point area. He only shot four midrange jumpers throughout his entire career in college. That meant that he did not rely a lot on an in-between game.

When it came to his playmaking, Trae Young did indeed lead the entire nation in assists and even tied an NCAA record of 22 assists in a single game. However, as the season progressed, it appeared that Young was someone who was willing to take gambles even though the passes looked impossible to make. His risk-taking tendencies led to over five turnovers a game. At one point, he even finished a game with 12 turnovers.

Young can thread the tough passes and make his teammates look good. But, at the same time, he could also be too careless with the ball and was forcing passes that were not even there. That is not something that would work at the NBA level as opposing teams can easily turn mistakes and turnovers into quick points.

With all his weaknesses taken into consideration, the biggest fear when it came to Trae Young was his inability to defend due to his lack of physical abilities at that end of the floor. Teams would be expected to focus on attacking Young's defensive weaknesses while capitalizing on his lack of strength and athleticism on both ends of the floor. Adding a bit of strength and working on his lateral quickness and defensive awareness might be able to help turn him into a better defender. Remember the fact that Chris Paul and Kyle Lowry are shorter than Trae Young but are both regarded as top-tier defenders at the point guard spot.

In any other case, Trae Young's other weaknesses such as his carelessness with the ball can be remedied with proper NBA-level training and coaching. But he was still too good of a prospect and too refined of a scorer to pass up. That was why, despite his lack of physical tools, he was still one of the top prospects of that draft, especially when the team looking to draft him needed some scoring punch from the point guard spot.

In the most optimistic of cases, Trae Young could potentially become the next Steph Curry, as he was simply a smaller and slightly quicker version of the two-time MVP. Yet again, the outlook at that time was that he was going to be a good starter who could provide his team some scoring at the NBA level. The safest projection was for him to become a quality starter, but not a lot of scouts believed he would become an instant star in the NBA.[v]

At the night of the draft, the Phoenix Suns selected Deandre Ayton with the first overall pick after telling the world prior to the draft that they were convinced that he was the best choice for the top overall pick. Next up, the Sacramento Kings selected Marvin Bagley because they needed a big man to play alongside their 2017 draft pick De'Aaron Fox, who was showing promise as a point guard.

With the third overall pick of the 2018 NBA Draft, the Atlanta Hawks were looking to add a potential star to their roster as they were trying to rebuild during an era where having an exceptional playmaker was the best way for a team to contend. They were looking at Luka Dončić, the Slovenian superstar who had just won the EuroLeague MVP, because he was arguably the best player left on the board.

Luka Dončić had previously worked out with the Atlanta Hawks and they loved what he brought to the table. At that point, the decision was for them to draft Dončić and keep him to help their rebuilding efforts. But, about an hour before the draft, the Dallas Mavericks called and offered a package they could not refuse. The Mavs wanted Luka and were willing to trade the fifth overall pick and a future first-round pick to make sure that the Hawks were going to give them what they wanted. For Atlanta, the offer seemed too attractive to pass up and they made the decision to draft Luka Dončić only to trade him to the Mavs.[vii]

The draft proceeded and the Memphis Grizzlies selected the young and versatile big man Jaren Jackson Jr. with the fourth overall pick. When it was time for the Dallas Mavericks to pick, they chose the player that the Atlanta Hawks wanted in exchange for Luka Dončić. Trae Young was selected fifth overall by the Dallas Mavericks but was traded to the Hawks in a move that initially seemed like a bad one for Atlanta.

Regardless of how it worked out for the two teams, Trae had just crossed out a goal on his list. He was finally an NBA player, a dream his father was never quite able to achieve but was diligent enough to help prepare his son for. But while making it this far was a goal for Trae Young, simply being an NBA player was not enough for someone with his mentality and hunger for greatness. Young's first step to becoming a star may have just been completed, but the next step for him was to work on his game and to make a big splash in the NBA.

Early Jitters, Race for Rookie of the Year

There were not a lot of expectations on Trae Young's shoulders when the Atlanta Hawks traded for him. After all, the Hawks were in the middle of a massive rebuild after what was a 24-win season the previous year. The last time they made the playoffs was in 2017 when they had former All-Stars Paul Millsap, Dwight Howard, and Kyle Korver leading a team that also had capable players Dennis Schroder and Tim Hardaway Jr. But that was a distant memory as they effectively fielded a new team during the 2017-18 season and failed to make any noise under former Coach of the Year Mike Budenholzer.

After parting ways with Budenholzer, the Hawks were coming into the 2018-19 season with a new coaching staff and a new core. The upcoming season was officially the start of a new era for the Hawks as most of the players that led the team to the postseason in 2017 were already in other franchises. With that, they were fielding a new group of young players and a core that was focused around young players John Collins and 2018, 19th-overall pick Kevin Huerter. Of course, it was Trae Young who was expected to lead the team into the future as their designated playmaker.

Luckily for Trae, he had a good mentor on that roster. The Atlanta Hawks brought in the league's elder statesman, Vince Carter, who was turning 42 years old in the middle of that season. Vince Carter may have been one of the greatest wingmen in the NBA during his prime, but the Hawks brought him in, not to give them a shot at the playoffs, but to work as a mentor for a team that had a lot of young and talented players. It was as if Carter worked as the father figure of the young Hawks.

Of course, it also helped that Carter was more than twice Young's age. He was drafted into the NBA before Trae was even born. And the funny part is, Vince Carter was about a year older than Trae Young's dad. That goes to show how much experience and wisdom the former All-Star had. It also made him the perfect mentor for the up-and-coming Trae Young.

Having a father figure who has seen and done almost everything in the NBA was something that helped Young's progression in the NBA. But, at that point, Young was still trying to adjust to the style of NBA play, just as he adjusted his game to suit the demands of his team when he transitioned from high school to college.

The transition, at least on the offensive side, did not come easy for Trae. He first saw action against NBA-level competition in the Summer League, where he was the most-watched player due to how impressive he was in college. However, he was also the most polarizing player in the league during that summer tournament as many naysayers were quick to throw criticisms at the young man.

Trae Young remained humble as a player despite how confident he always was on the floor, but he still got jeers from the crowd during the Summer League. Just about a year previously in college, he was shooting 30-foot shots and scoring 30 to 40 points a night. But in the summer prior to his debut in the NBA, he couldn't *buy* a bucket and fans were beginning to think that Young did not deserve the comparisons to Steph Curry. At one point, Trae Young was shooting only 25% from the floor overall and was barely making a fifth of the three-pointers he was attempting.[viii]

The problem during the Summer League was not that Young was missing his shots. Instead, it was because he was not able to get the looks he was capable of creating back when he was in college. As he struggled to create space between him and his defenders during the Summer League, it looked as if Trae Young truly did not know how far ahead NBA-level defenses were compared to college. This was when his lack of size and athleticism became apparent and he needed to rely more on his ball-handling and on his teammates to get the looks he needed to get off a shot.

As Trae continued to struggle during Summer League while getting criticized and booed by fans, some writers and analysts were quick to say that he should have just skipped the summer tournament to keep fans and opposing teams alike guessing on how good he really was. This was the route that Luka Dončić took as he decided to skip the 2018 Summer League right after the conclusion of the EuroLeague playoffs, wherein he led Real Madrid to the championship while winning both the season MVP and the Final Four MVP.

In Trae Young's case, skipping the Summer League might have been a good idea so that he could stay under the radar. But Young needed to play in the

Summer League to get himself acquainted with an entirely new type of playing field that was different from the one he was accustomed to in college. Going through the Summer League was sort of an adjustment period and a learning process for him. And because he was already so used to the attention he was getting from fans and media alike, he did not seem to mind the bad that came with all the hype.[viii]

For Trae Young, it was all about the next shot for him; he never really dwelled on the misses he had during the Summer League. Missing the last shot only meant another learning experience for him because he could use what he learned from that miss to focus more on the next play and the next shot. It was a slow and steady progression that even his teammate John Collins recognized when he told his rookie point guard that he needed to relax when things were happening so fast for him.

Trae Young might have struggled during the Summer League, but that was in no way a validation of what he was capable of in the NBA. A lot of players in the past have struggled in the Summer League for one reason or another while some players exploded in that tournament to win MVP honors. However, most of the Summer League MVPs did not have meaningful NBA careers. That only meant that the way a player performed during the Summer League did not exactly dictate the level of success he would have in the NBA. For some players like Trae Young, playing in that tournament was merely a way to adjust slowly to the way the NBA game is being played.

As expected, Trae Young did indeed carry on his Summer League struggles in the early portion of the 2018-19 regular season. He made his debut on October 17, 2018, in New York City against the Knicks. In that game, he finished with subpar numbers of 14 points, 6 rebounds, and 5 assists while shooting 5 out of 14 from the field. In the next game, he shot better when he went for 20 points and 9 assists. But his team fell to the Memphis Grizzlies by 14 points.

It was on October 21st, in a win over the Cleveland Cavaliers when Trae Young showcased a flash of brilliance. Playing against college rival Collin Sexton and the Cavs that had just recently lost LeBron James to the Los Angeles Lakers during free agency, Young destroyed the struggling team and went for 35 points and 11 assists while shooting 13 out of 23 from the field and 5 out of 14 from the three-point area. But such games seemed too rare for Young at that point as he was indeed struggling from the field while he was still adjusting to the style of play in the NBA.

Even though Trae was struggling to shoot in an entirely new and more competitive playing field, what did not change were his capabilities as a passing point guard. After scoring 24 points on 9 out of 13 shooting against Sacramento on Halloween, Young went for three consecutive double-double performances. His best during that run was when he finished a win against the Miami Heat with 24 points, 6 rebounds, and a new career-high of 15 assists.

Nevertheless, the struggle was still very much real. After those three consecutive double-doubles, Young went on three straight games that saw shooting a cumulative 7 out of 44 from the field. He made up for those games by going for 25 points and a new career-high of 17 assists in a loss to the Los Angeles Clippers on November 19th. But he still shot poorly from the three-point area in that game and only made a single shot out of five attempts.

During Trae Young's first 20 games in the NBA, it was apparent that he was still trying to adjust to the physicality, speed, and competitiveness of the greatest basketball league in the world. He averaged 15.7 points and 7.7 assists while shooting only 38.3% from the floor and 24% from the three-point area in those 20 games. Meanwhile, at that point in time, the young man he was traded for on draft night was already taking the league by storm while the top overall pick of his draft class was already averaging a double-double on points and rebounds.

While it was unfair to compare Trae Young to Deandre Ayton because the Hawks were not in the position to draft the center, people were quick to compare the young Oklahoma product to what Luka Dončić was already doing at that point in their respective careers. Dončić was showing his case for the Rookie of the Year Award early on because of how brilliant he already was as a rookie. This made fans and analysts alike wonder if it was really a smart move for the Hawks to give Dončić up to the Mavs in exchange for Trae Young.

Trae Young was certainly hearing the comparisons and criticisms. With all due respect to him, he was doing pretty well as a rookie, but what made it difficult for him was that he was getting compared to the player he was traded for on draft night as even Hawks fans were thinking what could have been had Atlanta decided to keep Dončić instead of trading him for Young. But the comparisons and criticisms did not dampen Trae Young's spirit.

He was still struggling as the season went by, but Trae Young was showing steady improvements in his game and approach. It was as if the game was slowing down for him while he was treating every game, every bad performance, and every missed shot, as learning experiences. During the entire month of December, Young's averages remained the same as what he had in his first 20 games but his shooting percentages improved to 43.1% and 34.7% in the 13 games he played that month.

After starting year 2019 with 5 points and 9 assists on January 2nd, Trae Young did not look back. He began his slow and steady rise as one of the finest rookies of his draft class after showing how much he had adjusted to the type of defenses he was seeing in the NBA. From then on, he only scored less than 10 points once. That happened on January 23rd when he finished the game with 5 points and 12 assists while shooting 1 out of 12 from the floor.

But after that dismal shooting performance on January 23rd, Trae Young looked like a house on fire. In what was arguably his best shooting performance at that point of the season, Young finished a loss to the Portland Trail Blazers (and Steph's brother, Seth Curry) with 30 points on 11 out of 15 shooting from the field. After that game, he went on to have four consecutive 20-point performances to average 26.8 points and 8.2 assists while shooting 53.5% from the floor and 43% from the three-point area in the five games he played from January 26th to February 2nd.

Averaging 17 points and 7.6 assists heading into the midseason All-Star break, Trae Young was still one of the finest rookies that season, even after such a slow start. He was chosen to take part in the 2019 Rising Stars Challenge as a member of Team USA. Los Angeles Lakers sophomore Kyle Kuzma may have won the MVP Award of that game but Trae Young was equally as impressive as he went for 25 points and 10 assists during the win for Team USA.

The break after the All-Star Weekend was all that Trae Young needed to get himself going and to right the ship he was steering. It was during the second half of the season—right after the All-Star break—that Trae Young proved to the world that he was not merely the guy that was traded for Luka Dončić. Instead, he became the young man who gave Dončić a run for his money for the Rookie of the Year Award because of how brilliantly he performed during the second half of the season.

In his first game back from the break, Young torched a Dončić-less Dallas Mavericks team in a loss. He finished that game with 30 points and 10 assists while making 5 out of 11 three-pointers he attempted. It was after that when he compiled together the best five-game run he had had at that point in his career. Trae went for 36 points and 8 assists while making a career-best 8 three-pointers in a win against the Houston Rockets on February 25th. Young followed that game two days later with 36 points, 8 rebounds, and 10 assists in what was nearly a triple-double in a win over the Minnesota Timberwolves.

Trae Young's best game at that point in his career happened on March 1st against the Chicago Bulls. That quadruple overtime game ranked as one of the greatest in recent memory as neither team was willing to give an edge to the other. It was Trae Young who was fueling Atlanta in that spirited performance after he played a total of 56 minutes while tallying a new career-high of 49 points to go along with 8 rebounds and 16 assists. Unfortunately, the Hawks ended up losing that game to the Bulls.

During that five-game run, Trae Young played like one of the finest players in the entire league. He averaged 34.8 points, 4.4 rebounds, and 10.4 assists while shooting 47% from the field and 49% from the three-point line. When people were quick to write Young off as someone whose game would probably never translate to the NBA, he was just as quick to work on his game and adjust to the style of play in the NBA.

Never known for being an all-around player, Trae Young recorded the first triple-double of his young career on March 9th. In that loss to the Brooklyn Nets, he finished with 23 points, 10 rebounds, and 11 assists. A few weeks later, he put together four straight games of at least 21 points and 11 assists. He averaged 27.3 points and 11.5 assists during that four-game stretch. And when the season was nearing its conclusion, Trae Young put together one last amazing performance to try to earn himself some votes for the Rookie of the Year Award. He finished a win over the Philadelphia

76ers on April 3rd with 33 points, 7 rebounds, and 12 assists.

At the conclusion of the regular season, Trae Young averaged 19.1 points, 3.7 rebounds, and a rookie-leading 8.1 assists in the 81 games he played and started in. He shot 41.8% from the field and 32.4% from the three-point line. Those numbers are indeed stellar for a rookie who was still adjusting to the NBA's style of play, but what was even more impressive was how Trae gradually went from a possible bust to one of the best rookies of his draft class.

In the 36 games that Trae Young played in 2018, he averaged 15.6 points on 39.6% from the field and 27.5% from the three-point area. Those are bad numbers for a player regarded as one of the best volume shooters to come out of the collegiate ranks in recent memory. However, Young eventually worked on his game and adjusted to the style of defenses he was seeing in the NBA. After averaging 17 points on 40.6% from the field and 31.2% from the three-point area in the 58 games before the All-Star break, Trae Young upped his numbers to 24.7 points and 9.2 assists while shooting 44.2% from the field and 34.8% from the three-point area in the 23 games he played after the midseason break. Those are All-Star numbers in anyone's book and Young was turning heads around with his fantastic performances after the All-Star Weekend.

The Atlanta Hawks, who won only 29 games that season, did not qualify for the playoffs. Their season may have ended when the regular season concluded, but Trae Young's season was not yet done. He had to wait for the annual NBA Awards, a show which was held right after the NBA Finals. And while he may have been written off early when he struggled to adjust to the NBA's style of defense, Young eventually became the only other rookie that could threaten Luka Dončić's claim to the Rookie of the Year Award.

Dončić's case for the Rookie of the Year award was a simple one. Scouts were doubting whether he could translate his game to the NBA because he did not have the athleticism and the quickness needed in the league's modern-day, pace-and-space style. However, when it came down to his skill, no one doubted what Luka could do as he was already one of the best professional basketball players in Europe at the age of 18.

The Mavs' young superstar could do it all. He could drive, finish, make tough layups, hit step-back jumpers, drill clutch three-pointers, rebound like a power forward, and pass like a point guard. His complete set of skills allowed him to average 21.2 points, 7.8 rebounds, and 6 assists. He led all rookies in points per game while finishing second rebounding and assists. As good as Dončić's all-around game was at the age of 19, it was his veteran savvy that made him an elite NBA player the moment he stepped onto the court.

Luka Dončić was already used to playing professional basketball because he started playing professionally against grown men when he was just 15 years old. At the time when Dončić was earning experience from the best basketball players that Europe had to offer, Trae Young was still torching high school basketball teams. In that regard, Dončić was far ahead of his class in terms of experience. It was like he was a five-year veteran in the body of a 6'7", 19-year old teenager. He was the perfect storm in terms of skill set and experience.

With Luka Dončić putting up huge numbers as a wingman playing point guard for the Dallas Mavericks, it was easy to say that he was the frontrunner for the Rookie of the Year Award. Plus, the kid had a magnetic smile and a love for the game of basketball that was attracting fans and media personalities over to his side. Some even said that he was going to win the Rookie of the Year Award unanimously. But that was only until Trae Young exploded in the second half of the season.

Trae Young's early-season struggles were well-documented. He had trouble finding a basket and seemingly did not have the range and the deep-ball accuracy that had scouts and analysts comparing him to the likes of Stephen Curry and Damian Lillard. No matter where he shot the ball from, he had trouble finding the bottom of the net. And when he tried to get to the basket, his lack of strength could not help him when finishing against bigger defenders. As such, Young got off to a poor start. But that did not dim the competitive fire he had in him.

Trae did not go through a lot of special training sessions and did not try to change his game a lot. Instead, he just merely adjusted to the grind of the NBA and to the style of defenses he was seeing. He kept on shooting the ball and he made it a point to focus on the next shot instead of dwelling on the dozens of misses he had in the past. It eventually clicked. He was making his baskets and was doing so at a high rate.

When he began to find his shooting stroke, defenses around the NBA were put on notice, as Trae Young was suddenly torching the league the same way he did back when he was in college. It became a norm for him to score 30 a game while shooting the ball at a respectable clip. The Steph Curry comparisons became understandable as Young was beginning to showcase the full arsenal of his offense. The way he ended the season as a scorer was remarkable and he became a serious contender for the Rookie of the Year Award just when the entire world thought that Dončić was going to win it unanimously.

On top of all of that, Trae Young may have struggled as a scorer early on but his playmaking remained consistent all season long. He was given the unenviable task of running the offense of a rebuilding

Atlanta Hawks team that did not have a lot of great players. But Young still managed to make everyone look good and formed a particularly good pick-and-roll relationship with rising big man John Collins. Young ended the season leading all rookies in assists with 8 per game while helping his teammates improve as scorers. Collins, in particular, fed off of Young's playmaking and ability to attract defenses and went on to improve his scoring average to 19.5 points on a 56% shooting clip. In that regard, Young may have already been the better playmaker compared to Dončić, who himself was already a very capable playmaker.

But the narratives also play a good role in determining NBA awards. The narrative for Dončić was that he was the league's wonderboy and was soon going to become the face of the NBA. He also had a fantastic start to the season and was able to finish his rookie campaign just as strong, averaging 22.7 points in the 17 games he played after the All-Star break.

Meanwhile, for Trae Young, the narrative was all about how he finished his rookie year strong after he pretty much had one of the worst starts a shooter can have. In his own words, the Rookie of the Year is a season-long award that needs to take into account how well the player performed not only at the start of the season but also at the end of it. And if you judged how well both Trae Young and Luka Dončić ended their seasons, you might actually give the nod to the Hawks' point guard because he was averaging 23.4 points and 9.3 assists since the start of February.[ix]

You could also take into account the stats that both those players had during certain stretches of the season. Luka Dončić started his first 39 games averaging 19.6 points and 4.9 assists but gradually improved his numbers when the Mavericks traded away Dennis Smith Jr. and he was given the point guard role. On the other hand, Trae Young ended his last 39 games with 22.7 points and 8.8 assists. So, if you judge it from that, you could argue that the Rookie of the Year race was closer than some people would say it was.

Shortly after the Toronto Raptors finished off the Golden State Warriors to win the 2019 NBA Championship, the awards show came. The Milwaukee Bucks' Giannis Antetokounmpo won the MVP Award over Houston's James Harden. Meanwhile, Rudy Gobert of the Utah Jazz was crowned the Defensive Player of the Year for two consecutive seasons.

For the Rookie of the Year Award, only two names truly stood out: Luka Dončić and Trae Young. With all due respect to Deandre Ayton, who was the only rookie to finish the season with a double-double after averaging 16.3 points and 10.3 rebounds, he simply did not have the kind of impact that both Dončić and Young had on the NBA.

But while Trae Young may have given the voters enough reason to vote for him when he finished his rookie campaign in the best possible way for a point guard, it was not enough. Young only earned himself two first-place votes and Luka Dončić received 98 out of a 100. Dončić won in a landslide victory for the Rookie of the Year Award but Trae Young put up a good fight and prevented the Slovenian sensation from becoming the sixth player in league history to win the award unanimously.

Trae Young and Luka Dončić. Those are two names that would forever be linked to one another because they were traded for one another in the 2018 NBA Draft and ended up becoming the two best rookies of their draft class. Media personalities and fans alike will always be talking about these two players side by side and will come up with hypothetical scenarios concerning the draft-day trade involving both Young and Dončić.

But, for all the comparisons, what-ifs, and non-existent rivalry that the media and fans were talking about,

Trae Young went on to say that the draft-day trade worked out well for them both. He recognized that both of them had spectacular rookie years while doing well for their respective teams' rebuilding stage.[x]

Still, at the end of it all, the competitive nature that drove Trae Young also led him to say that he was eventually going to end up becoming the better player ten years later.[x]

Well, who is to say that his statement cannot be true? There are plenty of things that can happen to change the narrative between Young and Dončić. In 2013, Lillard won the Rookie of the Year unanimously over Anthony Davis, but many would regard Davis as the better player today. Meanwhile, in 2014, Michael Carter-Williams won a landslide victory for the very same award but it is now Giannis Antetokounmpo who is the best player of that rookie class and even arguably the best player in the NBA. And in 2017, Malcolm Brogdon won the Rookie of the Year accolade but everybody knew that Joel Embiid was the better player.

A drastic improvement in Trae Young's game or a massive drop or plateau in Dončić's skill could possibly turn the tide in Young's favor later on. But no one can really say for certain what will happen in the future. But what is certain is that Trae Young is only going to get better and better. After all, with all the hard work he put himself through to get to the NBA, Young is only going to work harder to become one of the best players in the entire world.

Rise to Stardom

By virtue of their poor performance during the 2018-19 season and using the draft pick they got from the Luka Dončić trade a year ago, the Atlanta Hawks surrounded Trae Young with more talent by drafting the versatile forward and NCAA champion De'Andre Hunter as well as Duke shooting wingman Cam Reddish. The young Hawks just got even younger but they did a good job of providing Young with a gifted and rising core he could work with while he was working on his game.

Never one to slack off and spend the entire summer break resting or on the beach, Trae Young put in the necessary work that would help his transition from a Rookie of the Year runner-up to an actual All-Star player. One of the first things he did was join the Team USA Select team in preparation for the upcoming FIBA World Cup. However, while he had a good chance to make the team, he had to opt himself out due to a minor eye injury he suffered.[xi]

Trae Young did, however, still continue to work on his game after leaving the USA Basketball Select Team. The first thing he had on his list was to make sure he kept his body in top shape, not only by continuing to hit the weights but also by adding a few pounds to what was widely regarded as a slight and weak frame. Bulking up and adding at least 10 pounds of lean muscle was one of the right things for him to do so that he could keep up with bigger and stronger point guards on both ends of the floor while improving his ability to take contact on his way to the basket and finish strong against rim protectors.[xii]

But what was even more impressive was that Trae Young thought that he needed to add another dimension to what was already regarded as a complete offensive game for a shooting point guard. Back in his rookie year, about 65% of the shots that Young took were from the three-point line or within three feet from the basket. If you look at his efficiency, he was pretty respectable as a finisher between 3 and 10 feet away from the hoop because of the sweet floater he perfected back when he was in high school. Meanwhile, he also used his floater to shoot well from 10 to 16 feet as he shot about 45% from those distances. We all know his capabilities as a three-point shooter as he improved his efficiency from that area during the second half of his rookie year.

Simply put, the rookie version of Trae Young was essentially a layup or a three-pointer kind of person who occasionally shot a few close-range shots or floaters from time to time. Those are efficient shot selections in the NBA as far as the metrics and the advanced analytics were concerned. He would have been the perfect star player in a team like the Houston Rockets, who only wanted their players to shoot three-pointers or layups. But Trae Young believed he needed to diversify his offensive game if he wanted to take himself to the next level.

Trae Young did not attempt a lot of midrange jumpers as a rookie or even back in college (he only attempted four midrange shots his entire collegiate career). This part of his game was a reflection of how the NBA game now emphasizes more on shots that are considered efficient—the layups and the three-pointers. As a shooter, it was weird for Young to try to avoid taking midrange shots. And when he did shoot shots from beyond 16 feet, he only made 31.6% of those—

an indication that there was still a dimension in Young's shooting game that needed work.[xii]

The long midrange shot is regarded as the NBA's most inefficient shot if you just base it on the metrics and advanced analytics. At a time when the league is obsessed with what the numbers show, many teams favor layups and three-pointers and would rather dissuade their players from shooting the midrange shots. And while the midrange was never the hallmark of efficiency in the NBA, the eye test will tell you that this shot should be in the arsenal of some of the best players in the league.

Probably the reason why great players tend to have great midrange games is that this is a shot that defenses are most likely to give offenses just to make sure that they cover the three-point line and the paint. And when there is an open quality look within the perimeter, the great ones know how to capitalize on that.

That is why a lot of the great players over the past few years have excellent midrange shots. Players such as Michael Jordan, Kobe Bryant, LeBron James, Kevin Durant, Dwyane Wade, and Kawhi Leonard have won championships by developing and relying on their midrange games. The midrange shot might not be efficient, but it surely is a necessity for greatness.

In the NBA today, even the best point guards rely on the midrange shots. Curry goes for that shot occasionally, especially if the paint is clogged and his three-pointer is well covered. Kyrie Irving, one of the best isolation players in the league, relies on a steady diet of pull-up midrange shots after getting his defenders off-balance with his exceptional dribble moves. But arguably the best midrange point guard in the game is Chris Paul, who shoots that shot so efficiently that the Houston Rockets allowed him to take long two-pointers even though it was against their offensive philosophy.

All that said, Young was never going to be a hyper athlete like Russell Westbrook or a big point guard like John Wal. So, if Trae Young wanted to take the next step and add a weapon that opposing defenses are more likely to allow him to use, then he needed to develop his mid-range game. That was exactly his plan as he had already scheduled to work on his perimeter shot with the late great Kobe Bryant, who is regarded as probably the best to ever shoot the midrange shot alongside other familiar names such as Michael Jordan and Kevin Durant.[xii]

The offseason work for Trae Young was not merely for him to rely more on the midrange shot. For all accounts, his best weapon was still the three-pointer and his secondary weapon was his ability to get to the basket. Nevertheless, the purpose of working on the mid-range jumper was for him to be able to hit it with consistency when the shot was available. After all, the best players take the shots that they are given. And more often than not, they make those shots.

Other than training with Bryant in the offseason, Trae Young also spent time learning from another legend named Steve Nash. Young looked up many players while he was growing up. Many people regarded Steph Curry as his idol but Young actually spent more time watching Nash growing up because he was at the peak of his career when Trae was still in his formative years as a young boy. Young not only spent time watching Steve Nash on television but also made it a point to go to Oklahoma City Thunder games to catch the two-time MVP point guard whenever the Phoenix Suns were visiting.

What Trae Young loved about Steve Nash was that he was a lot like him in the sense that he played below the rim and had an above-average athleticism that made it seem like he did not belong in the NBA. But, then again, Nash dominated as a passing point guard and as a very efficient shooter despite the fact that he did not have the physical gifts of other NBA point guards.

It was during one of the Atlanta Hawks' road trips during the 2018-19 season when Trae Young first met Steve Nash after his head coach introduced the legendary point guard to the young up-and-coming playmaker. After that, they met again when they watched the 2019 UEFA Champions League in Europe. It was then and there when Nash agreed to work with the younger point guard.[xiii]

In Steve Nash, Trae Young had another mentor who could teach him how to shoot midrange jumpers more efficiently. Kobe Bryant was known more as a volume mid-range shooter who famously told the young Jayson Tatum to shoot as many jumpers as he could so long as he was confident enough that he could make them. Meanwhile, Nash himself was also regarded as one of the most efficient shooters in the history of the league after becoming the only player to make it to the 50-40-90 club four times. The trick was that Nash only shot the ball when he knew he could make the shot. This meant that Young had another angle to look at when learning how to become a better shooter in general.

Trae Young also learned the importance of knowing how to use angles from Steve Nash, who was famous for his high basketball IQ and his awareness of whatever was happening on the floor. Knowing how to use different angles on the floor is a unique gift that point guards need to harness if they want to become good scorers and terrific playmakers.

Generally speaking, Trae Young loved the experience he had with Steve Nash because he felt like they were cut from the same cloth in terms of skill set and physical gifts. In return, Steve Nash also went on to say that he believed Young had skills and talents so refined that he would not be surprised if he made the All-Star team sooner than later.[xiii] It turned out that Nash was right, as Young went on to have a stellar 2019-20 season.

Trae Young started the 2019-20 season with a win over the Detroit Pistons on October 24, 2019. Unlike the way he started his rookie year, he was efficient in this game and managed to hit 11 out of 21 from the field and 6 out of 10 from the three-point area to tally a total of 38 points on top of 7 rebounds and 9 assists. Proving that his first game that season was not a fluke, Young topped his performance by going for 39 points on 16 out of 25 from the field in a win over the Orlando Magic two days later.

It appeared that things had become different for Trae Young after putting himself through a lot of hard work during the offseason. On November 5th, he finished with his first double-double of the season when he went for 29 points and 13 assists in a win over the San Antonio Spurs. Three days later, he started what was to become four straight double-double performances. His best performance during that run was when he finished a win over the Denver Nuggets with 42 points and 11 assists. Overall, he averaged 32 points and 11.5 assists during that four-game run.

In a loss to the Toronto Raptors on November 23rd, Trae Young had his second career triple-double after going for 30 points, 10 rebounds, and 10 assists. He followed that game up with 37 points in a loss to the Minnesota Timberwolves. And on November 29th, he had his finest performance as a professional when he exploded with 49 points on 16 out of 28 shooting from the field and 7 out of 15 from the three-point line in a one-point loss to the Indiana Pacers.

Compared to last season when he started his first 20 games averaging about 16 points on a dismal shooting clip, Trae Young started his first 20 games of the 2019-20 season averaging 28.2 points and 8.3 assists while shooting over 45% from the field and 38.5% from the three-point area. It appeared that all the hard work had paid off for the young and rising point guard from Oklahoma.

After scoring 30 points in a loss to the Los Angeles Lakers on December 15th, Trae Young went for his third 40-point game of the season when he had 42 points against the New York Knicks in a loss. He followed that up with another 30-point output before going off for 47 points in a loss to the Brooklyn Nets on December 21st. He would then score 30 points and collect 11 assists against Cleveland two days later. During that five-game run of scoring at least 30 points, Young averaged 36 points, 6 rebounds, and 8 assists.

January 2020 was Trae Young's most explosive month at that point in his career. On January 4th he finished a win over the Indiana Pacers with 41 points. Four days later, he torched James Harden and the Houston Rockets for his first 40-point triple-double after he went for 42 points, 13 rebounds, and 10 assists in a loss for the Atlanta Hawks. On January 20th, Young had his third 40-point game of that month when he went for 42 points and 15 assists.

On January 26, 2020, tragedy struck when it was announced that basketball legend Kobe Bryant, his second daughter Gianna Bryant, and seven other passengers were killed in a helicopter crash in Southern California while they were on their way to a basketball camp. The entire world was in shock and many NBA players were saddened by the loss of one of the all-time greats the game has ever seen.

Different players and teams paid their own respective tributes to the most inspiring and most popular figure basketball has seen in the post-Jordan era. For Trae Young, he wore Kobe's number 8 jersey in the first 8 seconds of the game. He also scored 45 points and recorded 14 assists in a win over the Washington Wizards during that tragic day. Young, after the game, told reporters that he felt Kobe's presence in that performance. For him, Kobe was his Michael Jordan and was someone he looked up to considering that his confidence level was so similar to that of Bryant's "Mamba Mentality." He then promised that Kobe's memory would live on in his game and in the games of the other players he inspired.^{xiv}

Overall, during the month of January, Trae averaged 31.7 points, 5.3 rebounds, and 11.5 assists while shooting 45% from the field and 37.5% from the three-point area. The month of January also imparted a blessing to Trae Young. It was on January 23rd when he found out that he was selected to take part in the 2020 All-Star Game as an All-Star for the Eastern Conference. But the most amazing part about that was that the entire world voted him in as a starter. Young became the first Hawks starter for an All-Star Game since Dikembe Mutombo did it 22 years ago—before Trae was even born.

The All-Star nod was a validation of the hard work that Trae Young had himself gone through, not only in the last offseason but throughout his entire life. Undersized and often seen as an underdog due to his lack of physical gifts, Trae Young was an All-Star starter in just his second season in the NBA and at the tender age of 21. When he received the news that he was selected as a starter, he could not contain his happiness and emotion as he burst into tears. The Atlanta Hawks may not have been in playoff contention at that point, but Young deserved that accolade just as much as any other All-Star starter did.

Knowing that he had already worked hard enough to be considered one of the best players in the entire league, Young went for 48 points and 13 assists in a win over the New York Knicks on February 9th. And right before suiting up for Chicago to take part in the All-Star Weekend, Trae Young finished a loss to the Cleveland Cavaliers with 27 points and 12 assists.

The All-Star Weekend was Trae Young's coming out party in the NBA as he participated in all three days. First off, he started for Team USA in the Rising Stars Challenge. He scored 18 points and had 7 assists to help lead his team against Team World. Young even had a spectacular moment with Luka Dončić when the halftime clock was just about to end and the Slovenian guard was still in the backcourt.

Young was defending Dončić but he playfully told his Rookie of the Year rival to shoot the ball all the way from half-court. Dončić did so, and Trae and Luka stood side by side smiling while waiting for the result of the shot. Dončić made the shot and the two youngsters, barely out of their teenage years, could not help but laugh together. When the entire world thought that there was a rivalry between Trae Young and Luka Dončić because of how they were often compared to one another, they went on to show that they were merely kids enjoying the limelight and the opportunity to play against one another as friends and colleagues.

Dončić, like Young, was also selected as a starter for the Western Conference All-Stars and had risen to the level of an MVP candidate that season. And during the All-Star Game, Trae Young started as a member of

Team Giannis and finished with 10 points and 10 assists in a loss to Team LeBron. Meanwhile, Luka finished with only 8 points while starting for the winning team.

Bolstered by the excitement of making his first All-Star appearance, Trae Young went back to work on February 20th to put on a show against the Miami Heat. In that game, he finished with a career-high of 50 points while making 12 of his 25 shots and 8 of his 15 three-point attempts. And after that game, he went for five straight games of recording at least 20 points and 10 assists to average 27.4 points and 12 assists from February 22nd to the 29th.

On March 9th, Trae Young finished with another spectacular performance as a point guard when he went for 31 points and 16 assists in a win over the Charlotte Hornets. He followed that up with 42 points and 11 assists against the New York Knicks in a loss in what appeared to be his final game for that season, not because of an injury, but because of a worldwide crisis.

At the start of the year 2020, news broke out that there was a new coronavirus (COVID-19) that was first detected in Wuhan, China late in 2019 and was spreading all over the world like wildfire because of how rapid its transmission rate was. As the months went by, it appeared that the world was unable to contain the virus as it reached all the way to the United States and started to spread as quickly as it did in China. On March 13th, the Utah Jazz's Rudy Gobert tested positive for COVID-19.

Knowing how dangerous the virus is and how quickly it can be transmitted from one person to another, NBA Commissioner Adam Silver announced that the 2019-20 NBA season would have to be suspended indefinitely until the dust has already cleared out.[xv] The NBA, the sporting world, and the entire world in general had to be halted as there was a need to combat and stop the spread of the infectious epidemic.

No one knew for certain when or if the NBA season would restart. But, for all intents and purposes, Trae Young's second season in the league halted in the most unfortunate of ways as everyone in the NBA understood the gravity of the situation. In the 60 games he played that season, Young averaged improved numbers of 29.6 points, 4.3 rebounds, and 9.3 assists while shooting 43.7% from the field and 36.1% from the three-point area. He ended his season fourth in scoring behind James Harden, Bradley Beal, and Giannis Antetokounmpo. Young was also scoring and assisting more than Luka Dončić that season, although the latter was rebounding a lot more.

Playing for the 20-47 Atlanta Hawks, Trae Young's regular season was already done, regardless of whether or not the 2019-20 season was going to resume. The Hawks were in no shape to make it to the playoffs and were only going to play for experience if the season were to resume. But that did not mean that Trae Young's shortened season ended up as a waste. He proved during that season that he was just as good as advertised when he came out of college. On top of that, he became his own player and was seemingly not just a Stephen Curry clone but an entirely different player in his own right. As young as he was when his second season ended abruptly, Trae Young still has a long way to go before he will truly reach elite status, not only as an individual but also as a winner.

Chapter 5: Personal Life

Trae Young was born into a basketball family as his father Rayford Young played four years of college basketball as a point guard. In fact, Rayford was in the middle of his junior year when Trae was born. After his collegiate career, the elder Young spend several years playing professionally in Europe while the toddler Young tagged along to watch his father play games in many different European countries.

The eldest of four, Trae Young has three other siblings namely Caitlyn, Camryn, and Timothy. Trae's youngest brother Tim was still in elementary school when the All-Star point guard first started his career in the NBA. Trae also considers himself a family man and is more likely to spend quality time with his family than to go out with friends during his free time. Indeed, his decision to go to the University of Oklahoma was partly due to the fact that he wanted to stay close to his family during college.

Other than spending time at home with his family, Trae Young is also somewhat of a laidback person, someone used to the slow and rural life in a small town such as Norman, Oklahoma. When he is not playing basketball or training in the gym, Young is most likely at home watching movies and playing video games as any other laidback young man would.[xvi]

Growing up during the 2000s and the early part of the 2010s, Trae Young had a number of players that he looked up to. He spent a lot of time watching Russell Westbrook play in the Thunder because of how close Oklahoma City was to his hometown. Trae also enjoyed looking at plays and training sessions of the likes of Kyrie Irving and Stephen Curry, both of whom are players his style of play resembles.

Even though Young has been defined as "the next coming of Stephen Curry," he has spent a considerable amount of time emulating Steve Nash because Nash was his most-revered idol when he was still a young boy. Trae spent a lot of time studying Nash's game and he even patterned his floater after the two-time MVP point guard. Young also considers Kobe Bryant as the Michel Jordan of his era and he also tries to emulate the late legend's Mamba Mentality and supreme confidence.

Chapter 6: Legacy and Future

As young as Trae Young is, he still has a long way to go before you could truly say that he has had an impact or created a lasting legacy in the NBA, or even in the world of basketball in general. But, because he is one of the rapidly-rising stars in the league today, he can be considered as one of the banner carriers of legacies heading into the future.

Playing for the Atlanta Hawks as the cornerstone of the franchise, Trae Young has the makings of the team's newest superstar. The Hawks have had a lot of All-Stars over the past two decades. This includes Joe Johnson, Paul Millsap, and Al Horford. But not since the time of Dominique Wilkins has Atlanta seen a player with the makings of becoming a superstar. In fact, the last time Atlanta had a player good enough to start in the All-Star Game was in 1998 when center Dikembe Mutombo was selected as a starter. After that, the Hawks have had quality All-Stars but the team never had a player with the talent and potential of someone who could potentially become a top 10 star in the league.

Then came Trae Young, who effectively became the centerpiece of the Atlanta Hawks' rebuilding efforts. When Young was drafted, he was expected to become an All-Star. But not a lot of people thought that he was actually capable of becoming a player that could average 30 points and 10 assists at any given time. He did that as early as his second year when he improved his numbers to average 29 points and 9 assists. As such, Trae Young became the first Hawks All-Star starter since 1998.

Because of how quickly he was able to rise to the level of an All-Star starter, Young is now arguably the most talented star the Hawks has seen in the last three decades. He has a magnetic personality and the charisma of a superstar and is undoubtedly the standard-bearer of the entire franchise heading into the future. That is why the Atlanta Hawks did not mind too much that they traded Luka Dončić in exchange for a player who has the potential to become one of the greatest point guards of his generation.

Speaking of point guards, Trae Young is on his way to becoming one of the best playmakers of his generation. As of this writing, names such as Stephen Curry, Russell Westbrook, Kyrie Irving, and Damian Lillard are still the top names at the point guard spot. However, Young can potentially become just as great as those players and could perhaps have a better career than his predecessors. After all, much of what Young has in his arsenal is thanks to the inspirational, talented point guards of the past and present.

If you look at the way Trae Young plays, he will resemble a lot of players of the past and present. He was marketed as the next coming of Stephen Curry because of how he could shoot from a distance, but he has proven himself to be more than just a Curry clone.

He handles the ball like Kyrie Irving and also has his shiftiness. He could make plays for others like a Steve Nash and has a sweet floater patterned after the two-time MVP's own floater. Young also has the cold-blooded mentality that has always been evident in the way Damian Lillard plays.

With all due respect to the past and present point guards, Trae Young has become so good that he is effectively the conglomeration of all the unathletic and sweet-shooting playmakers of the 2010s. He may not have the size and speed of a John Wall or the nuclear athletic capabilities of a Russell Westbrook, but Trae Young has proven himself more than ready and capable of carrying the point guard spot to an entirely new level heading into the future.

And when it comes to Trae Young's future, it may be difficult to judge how far he will go, not because the future is uncertain but because this young man is one of the game's hardest workers. He has already crossed

All-Star starter off his to-do list and has several more personal and team goals to go. After all, he is yet to prove himself as a winner after spending two losing seasons with the Atlanta Hawks.

Trae Young is by no means a perfect player. He still has a lot of room left to grow. For one, his defense is still his most glaring weakness. He could also improve his accuracy from the floor and become a shooter efficient enough to make the elite 50-40-90 club. But, as of now, the sky is still the limit for this talented and hardworking star point guard.

Making the playoffs, winning an MVP, getting named to an All-NBA team, and possibly winning a championship are still goals that Trae Young has yet to achieve. But if we were to judge his chances at those based on how quickly he has risen through the ranks and how hard he is working on his game, there is a pretty good possibility that he may one day become an elite player and even a champion.

Final Word/About the Author

I was born and raised in Norwalk, Connecticut. Growing up, I could often be found spending many nights watching basketball, soccer, and football matches with my father in the family living room. I love sports and everything that sports can embody. I believe that sports are one of most genuine forms of competition, heart, and determination. I write my works to learn more about influential athletes in the hopes that from my writing, you the reader can walk away inspired to put in an equal if not greater amount of hard work and perseverance to pursue your goals. If you enjoyed *Trae Young: The Inspiring Story of One of Basketball's Star Guards,* please leave a review! Also, you can read more of my works on *Serena Williams, Rafael Nadal, Roger Federer, Novak Djokovic, Richard Sherman, Andrew Luck, Rob Gronkowski, Brett Favre, Calvin Johnson, Drew Brees, J.J. Watt, Colin Kaepernick, Aaron Rodgers, Peyton Manning, Tom Brady, Russell Wilson, Gregg*

Popovich, Pat Riley, John Wooden, Steve Kerr, Brad Stevens, Red Auerbach, Doc Rivers, Erik Spoelstra, Michael Jordan, LeBron James, Kyrie Irving, Klay Thompson, Stephen Curry, Kevin Durant, Russell Westbrook, Anthony Davis, Chris Paul, Blake Griffin, Kobe Bryant, Joakim Noah, Scottie Pippen, Carmelo Anthony, Kevin Love, Grant Hill, Tracy McGrady, Vince Carter, Patrick Ewing, Karl Malone, Tony Parker, Allen Iverson, Hakeem Olajuwon, Reggie Miller, Michael Carter-Williams, John Wall, James Harden, Tim Duncan, Steve Nash, Draymond Green, Kawhi Leonard, Dwyane Wade, Ray Allen, Pau Gasol, Dirk Nowitzki, Jimmy Butler, Paul Pierce, Manu Ginobili, Pete Maravich, Larry Bird, Kyle Lowry, Jason Kidd, David Robinson, LaMarcus Aldridge, Derrick Rose, Paul George, Kevin Garnett, Chris Paul, Marc Gasol, Yao Ming, Al Horford, Amar'e Stoudemire, DeMar DeRozan, Isaiah Thomas, Kemba Walker, Chris Bosh, Andre Drummond, JJ Redick, DeMarcus Cousins, Wilt Chamberlain, Bradley Beal,

Rudy Gobert, Aaron Gordon, Kristaps Porzingis, Nikola Vucevic, Andre Iguodala, Devin Booker, John Stockton, Jeremy Lin, Chris Paul, Pascal Siakam, Jayson Tatum, Gordon Hayward, Nikola Jokic, Bill Russell, Victor Oladipo, Luka Doncic, Ben Simmons, Shaquille O'Neal, Joel Embiid, Donovan Mitchell, Damian Lillard and Giannis Antetokounmpo in the Kindle Store. If you love basketball, check out my website at claytongeoffreys.com to join my exclusive list where I let you know about my latest books and give you lots of goodies.

Like what you read? Please leave a review!

I write because I love sharing the stories of influential athletes like Trae Young with fantastic readers like you. My readers inspire me to write more so please do not hesitate to let me know what you thought by leaving a review! If you love books on life, basketball, or productivity, check out my website at claytongeoffreys.com to join my exclusive list where I let you know about my latest books. Aside from being the first to hear about my latest releases, you can also download a free copy of *33 Life Lessons: Success Principles, Career Advice & Habits of Successful People*. See you there!

Clayton

References

[i] Greene, Dan. "How Trae Young transformed Oklahoma while doing the unprecedented". *Sports Illustrated*. 7 February 2018. Web.

[ii] "A Trae Young throwback, looking back at a journey to the NBA". *Kfor.com*. 5 August 2018. Web.

[iii] Williams, Aaron. "High school report card: Trae Young". *Maxpreps*. 19 June 2018. Web.

[iv] *ESPN*. Web.

[v] Wasserman, Jonathan. "Trae Young NBA draft 2018: Scouting report for Atlanta Hawks' pick". *Bleacher Report*. 22 June 2018. Web.

[vi] *NBAdraft.net*. Web.

[vii] Kozlowski, Joe. "Why did the Atlanta Hawks trade Luka Dončić to Dallas?". *Sportscasting*. Web.

[viii] Powell, Shaun. "Summer League no place to label Trae Young's game, potential in the NBA". *NBA.com*. 10 July 2018. Web.

[ix] Zillgitt, Jeff. "NBA Rookie of the Year: Surging Trae Young makes case against front-runner Luka Dončić". *USA Today*. 5 April 2019. Web.

[x] Zucker, Joseph. "Trae Young says Luka Dončić trade 'worked out' for both Hawks and Mavericks". *Bleacher Report*. 29 January 2019. Web.

[xi] "Minor injury forces Trae Young to leave USA Basketball Select Team". *NBA.com*. 8 August 2019. Web.

[xii] Quinn, Sam. "Hawks' Trae Young bulks up, plans to work with Kobe Bryant on mid-range game after Team USA training camp, per report". *CBS Sports*. 31 July 2019. Web.

[xiii] Spears, Marc J. "Trae Young gets schooled by Steve Nash: 'It's all about what he sees on the court'". *The Undefeated*. 16 October 2019. Web.

[xiv] Siddiqi, DJ. "Hawks' Trae Young remembers Kobe Bryant, calls Lakers great his 'Jordan'". *Clutchpoints*. 24 February 2020. Web.

[xv] Rohlin, Melissa. "NBA Commissioner Adam Silver says suspension will last at least 30 days". *Sports Illustrated*. 13 March 2020. Web.

[xvi] Gustashaw, Megan. "The making of an outfit and an athlete: Trae Young". *Express*. Web.

Made in the USA
Middletown, DE
26 September 2021